Heal

Over

Time

Healing Through Love and Forgiveness

Nikki Natasha Hunter

Heal Over Time

Heal Over Time

ISBN: 979-8-9895154-3-1
LCCN: 2023922199

Heal Over Time

~ A Heartfelt Dedication to Generations Past and Future ~

This book is dedicated to my beloved sons, daughters, grandchildren, nieces, nephews, and all the children yet to come.

Praise for The Intentional Healer

It takes great courage and strength to acknowledge one's mistakes and actively work towards a better path. Choosing to prioritize love and forgiveness in this journey is a powerful tool for personal growth and healing. By letting go of anger and resentment, we free ourselves from the weight of negativity and open ourselves up to new opportunities and experiences. It's important to remember that change is a process and it won't happen overnight, but with determination, kindness, and self-reflection, we can create a brighter future for ourselves and those around us. So let us celebrate those who choose to walk the path of love and forgiveness and support them in their journey towards a happier and more fulfilling life.

Table of Content

Heal Over Time

Heal Over Time

Introduction
The Power of Reflecting on Life Experiences

My life's journey has been full of twists and turns. I was an aunt before I was born. I became a teenage mother of twins, but I was determined to succeed. I graduated and became a certified nurses aide, then transitioned to a customer service job with a telecommunications company. I worked my way up to become a corporate Instructor, but unfortunately, the company went under, and I was laid off. Undeterred, I went back to school, earned a BA in Psychology, and became a Police Officer. After becoming a Sgt., my husband's promotion led us to relocate to GA. There, I became a holistic coach, doula, and non-profit leader in my community. I serve on the board of several non-profits, each with different areas of need, such as internships and marketing. Over the years, I have earned numerous awards, but my most fulfilling role is being a stay-at-home mother, homeschooling my children, and watching them blossom.

Over the span of 32 years, I have been blessed with the opportunity to give birth multiple times. Three of my children were born over ten years apart, a unique experience that allowed me to gain valuable knowledge and wisdom from observing my adult children as they navigate through life. By watching them closely, I have witnessed their successes, failures, lessons learned, and even death. This unique perspective has allowed me to reflect on my own parenting style and adapt it to better suit the needs of my youngest children. Through my experiences, I have discovered the importance of forgiveness, love, patience, understanding, and the power of time.

During my early years, I learned the hard way that prioritizing material possessions over spending time with my children was a trap. With today's fast-paced and materialistic society, we often find ourselves working long hours to provide for our families. Yet, we may feel guilty and try to make up for lost time by buying our children the latest gadgets, toys, or designer clothing. However, children need the love, attention, and guidance of their parents more than material wealth. Quality time spent together is essential for building strong relationships, promoting emotional growth, and instilling important values in children. Engaging in meaningful conversations, playing games, or participating in activities are all great ways to bond with your children. Remember, prioritizing quality time with your children over material possessions is essential to ensure their overall well-being and happiness. I learned over time that time is more valuable than any material possession.

We are all connected, and I hope to start a spiritual conversation with the world that I haven't had a chance to. I believe that everyone has wisdom and happiness within them, and it is important to find ways to share and spread it. Through my life, I have learned about the butterfly effect – as the one that was touched, I reached out to touch others. The love you show to one plant can grow a garden.

Family dysfunction can be deeply rooted in a group of people. Breaking the cycle of dysfunction within a family unit requires a strong commitment to doing things differently. It is not enough to just try, but one must actively engage in new behaviors and patterns. This commitment means recognizing and acknowledging the dysfunctional patterns that have been ingrained within the family and making a conscious effort to break free from them. It requires a willingness to change, challenge old beliefs and habits, and embrace healthier ways of relating and communicating. By committing to doing things differently, individuals within the family unit can create a positive shift, breaking free from the cycle of dysfunction and creating a healthier and more harmonious family dynamic.

I had to step away from what felt familiar to me in order to explore and learn new ideas that I can now share to enhance the overall well-being of others. By stepping out of your comfort zone and engaging with different perspectives, you open yourself up to a world of endless possibilities. Learning new ideas from various sources helps you gain a broader understanding of life and enables you to think critically. The insights gained can be brought back to your family, fostering innovation and growth. Introducing fresh perspectives and innovative solutions can help improve a family's coping abilities and more. Embracing new ideas ultimately leads to a more vibrant and successful collective family. Therefore, breaking away from habits that have bound us to ideologies that did not serve growth to learn and grow individually is not only beneficial for personal development but also for the betterment of the entire family.

As we journey through life, we encounter a wide range of experiences that shape our perceptions and beliefs. It is important to remember that everyone's journey is unique, and we can all learn from each other's experiences. By sharing our stories and perspectives, we can foster a deeper sense of understanding and empathy, which can ultimately lead to a more connected and compassionate world.

In this book, I hope to share some of my own experiences and insights in the hopes that they may be helpful or inspiring to others. Whether you are a parent, a child, or simply someone who is interested in personal growth and development, I believe that there is something in this book for everyone.

Above all else, I believe in the power of love and forgiveness. No matter what challenges we may face, these two qualities can help us to overcome even the toughest obstacles and find a sense of peace and happiness in our lives. I hope that by sharing my own experiences and insights, I can help others to find their own path towards healing, growth, and happiness..

Chapter 1

Navigating Life's Many Roles and Priorities

Instead of telling others who we are and how we operate, we should show them through our actions. In fact, we could even ask them who we are to them to gain more insight. Throughout our lives, we encounter various roles that may seem intimidating at first. It's easy to feel overwhelmed when faced with new and unfamiliar responsibilities. However, it's important to remember that each role serves a unique purpose and requires different skills and perspectives.

For instance, a role as a daughter may require us to seek guidance from our parents and provide support, while being a mother-in-law may demand patience and understanding as we embrace new family members. As we grow, we may transition from being a student to a mentor, or from a caregiver to a patient. Our understanding of these roles is shaped by our upbringing, and our experiences with family members, such as parents, siblings, grandparents, aunts, or uncles. The absence of a significant role model in our lives can be as harmful as a negative one, causing childhood trauma and leaving us unprepared for future responsibilities.

To gain perspective on your place in life, consider this scenario: You and your son or daughter-in-law are both hanging from a cliff, and your son or daughter has only one second to choose whom to save. While you don't know what she or he would do, you would let go because you wouldn't want them to bear such a burden. Instead, you would want them to lead a happy life with their spouse and raise their children together, just as you did. Though you may survive the fall, that's not the point. The crucial point is to recognize your position in time and make the right decisions that align with your values. While unfamiliar situations can be daunting, it's up to each of us to put in the effort and select the best course of action for the situation at hand.

By embracing our different roles, we can develop deeper relationships and find satisfaction in the unique contributions we make to the world around us. Although adapting to new roles and changes can be challenging, it's important to remain open-minded and adaptable. Every role is an opportunity to learn and grow, and to find joy in the diversity of life's experiences.

Our priorities are also subject to change as we grow and experience different stages of life. In childhood, we may focus on pleasing our parents and earning their approval. As we become parents ourselves, our focus shifts to providing for and nurturing our own children, and ensuring they have the best possible start in life. Once our children leave home, our priorities may change again, this time towards nurturing our relationship with our spouse or partner. With more free time and fewer responsibilities, we may find ourselves able to focus on what truly matters and invest in our most important relationships.

It's crucial to recognize that our priorities are fluid and can change over time. By staying open to new experiences and willing to adapt to different circumstances, we can continue to grow and thrive, no matter what life throws our way.

It's also important to remember that our roles and priorities are not set in stone. Sometimes we may find that a particular role or responsibility is no longer serving us, or that it's time to make a change. It can be difficult to let go of something that has been a part of our identity for a long time, but it's important to have the courage to make the necessary adjustments when the time comes.

For example, we may realize that we are no longer fulfilled in our career and decide to pursue a new path. Or we may find that a relationship is no longer serving us and choose to end it. It can be scary to make these changes, but it's important to remember that we have the power to shape our lives in a way that brings us happiness and harmony.

As we navigate through life's different roles and priorities, it's important to remember to be kind and patient with ourselves. We may not always get it right the first time, and that's okay. Each experience is an opportunity to learn and grow. It's also important to surround ourselves with a supportive community of friends and family who can help guide us through life's ups and downs.

In addition to our personal roles and priorities, it's important to also consider our larger impact on the world around us. We all have the power to make a positive difference in the lives of others, whether it's through volunteering, activism, or simply being kind and compassionate towards those we encounter. By using our unique skills and perspectives to contribute to the greater good, we can create a better world for ourselves and future generations.

Overall, navigating life's different roles and priorities can be a challenging but rewarding journey. By staying true to ourselves, adapting to change, and embracing new experiences, we can create a life that is full of purpose, joy, and gratification.

Heal Over Time

Chapter 2

The Importance of Positive Role Models for Children and Adults Alike

Children who witness real-life examples of success are more likely to grow and develop positively. They gain valuable insights into the key qualities and traits that lead to achievement by observing successful individuals. Real-life examples demonstrate the hard work, determination, and perseverance required to reach one's goals, motivating children to set their own aspirations and work towards them. Additionally, witnessing others' success fosters a sense of possibility and confidence within children, encouraging them to believe in their own potential. When children see that success is attainable, they are motivated to strive for excellence in their own lives. Furthermore, real-life examples of success provide children with role models to emulate and learn from, instilling important values such as discipline, resilience, and dedication. In short, exposing children to real-life examples of success is crucial in shaping their aspirations, boosting their self-confidence, and equipping them with the necessary tools for a bright future.

Childhood connections often form the strongest bonds within families for several reasons. During childhood, individuals are more receptive to forming deep emotional ties, without external factors that can potentially strain relationships. Shared experiences and memories created during childhood form a strong foundation for family connections. Siblings and cousins growing up together develop a unique understanding and familiarity, leading to unconditional support and an ability to navigate challenges. The guidance and support received from parents and other family members during this period shape individuals' perspectives on family, fostering a sense of loyalty and commitment.

As individuals transition into adulthood, their priorities shift, and they may not have as much time to devote to maintaining relationships with extended family members. Despite this, those early childhood connections can remain strong and provide a source of comfort and stability throughout life's ups and downs. For many people, family is where they find their sense of belonging, and the bonds formed in childhood can be instrumental in creating that feeling.

In a world that can feel increasingly disconnected, the enduring connections of family offer a unique and invaluable source of support and love. Whether it's through regular phone calls, visits, or simply reminiscing about old times, maintaining those childhood connections can help individuals stay grounded and connected to their roots. Ultimately, the bonds formed in childhood can provide a foundation for a lifetime of love and connection within the family. As parents, it's important to recognize the value in investing time to establish these connections.

However, not everyone has had great role models while growing up or opportunities to connect with family. In such cases, it is the individual's responsibility to seek out positive family members and role models now. One can start by defining what they consider to be a good father or mother and then find a mentor who fits the description. Observing other families and taking notes on the successful characteristics they demonstrate is a useful exercise.

Defining family roles is crucial for avoiding conflicts and misunderstandings while fostering a sense of unity and cooperation. In addition to defining family roles, it is also important to have positive role models to look up to. These role models can be family members, friends, or even public figures. By observing and learning from these individuals, family members can develop important qualities such as empathy, kindness, and resilience.

Finding role models can be a fun and rewarding process. Encouraging family members to share their role models with each other and discussing what they admire about them can help to strengthen the family bond and create a supportive environment for personal growth and development.

Having positive role models is beneficial not just to children, but to individuals of all ages. They can provide guidance, support, and inspiration, helping individuals to stay motivated and focused on their goals. Role models can also offer valuable insights and advice based on their own experiences, helping to navigate challenges and overcome obstacles.

In today's digital age, finding positive role models has become easier than ever through social media, online communities, and networking platforms. By actively seeking out and learning from positive role models, individuals can enhance their personal and professional development and achieve greater success in all areas of life.

In conclusion, having positive role models can greatly impact personal growth and development. By seeking out individuals who exemplify the qualities and traits one aspires to have, one can enhance their personal and professional lives and achieve greater success. It is an ongoing process, and we should always be open to learning from others and expanding our horizons.

Define family roles that you feel like you haven't had and find a role model in your community that you can learn from. We must first seek out an understanding of what a good parents looks like. Each member of the family can develop an understanding of their role and responsibilities within their family by listening to what others members would like from them. This not only helps to avoid conflicts and misunderstandings, but also fosters a sense of unity and cooperation.

In addition to defining family roles, it is also important to have positive role models to look up to. These role models can be family members, friends, or even public figures. By observing and learning from these individuals, family members can develop important qualities such as empathy, kindness, and resilience.

Finding role models can be a fun and rewarding process. Encourage family members to share their role models with each other and discuss what they admire about them. This can help to strengthen the family bond and create a supportive environment for personal growth and development.

It is never too late to find positive role models, no matter what age you are. Seeking out individuals who exemplify the qualities and traits you aspire to have can be a powerful tool for personal growth and development. Role models can provide guidance, support, and inspiration, helping you to stay motivated and focused on your goals. They can also offer valuable insights and advice based on their own experiences, helping you to navigate challenges and overcome obstacles. In today's digital age, it is easier than ever to find role models through social media, online communities, and networking platforms. By actively seeking out and learning from positive role models, you can enhance your own personal and professional development and achieve greater success in all areas of your life.

It is important to note that having role models is not just beneficial to children, but to individuals of all ages. The benefits of having positive role models extend beyond childhood and can greatly impact personal and professional growth. Role models can provide guidance, support, and inspiration, helping individuals to stay motivated and focused on their goals. They can also offer valuable insights and advice based on their own experiences, helping to navigate challenges and overcome obstacles.

In today's fast-paced world, finding positive role models can be a daunting task for some. However, with the advent of technology and social media, it has become easier than ever to seek out and connect with individuals who can serve as positive influences in our lives. From online communities to networking platforms and mentorship programs, there are many resources available for individuals looking to find role models and build meaningful relationships with them.

In conclusion, whether it is for children or adults, having positive role models can greatly impact personal growth and development. By seeking out individuals who exemplify the qualities and traits we aspire to have, we can enhance our own personal and professional lives and achieve greater success. It is important to remember that finding role models is an ongoing process, and we should always be open to learning from others and expanding our horizons.

Chapter 3
Shaping the Character of the Next Generation

Our behavior and actions as adults have a significant impact on children. Teaching our children to appreciate the small things in life sets them up to appreciate the big things. We allow them to set their scale of appreciation at zero. I like to call it appreciating the grape seed so they can eventually appreciate the watermelon. Our existence is due to our creator and then our parents. If we can't show an ounce of appreciation for that regardless of any further action, what are we teaching our children? We want our children to honor us, but we first must honor our parents regardless of any mistakes they have made. Forgive their shortcomings and appreciate the grape seed. You can appreciate your life and move forward from there.

Children are observant and often emulate the behavior they see in adults. Therefore, it is crucial for us to set a positive example by demonstrating respect, kindness, and integrity. By showing empathy and compassion, we teach children how to treat others with love and understanding. Our demeanor and attitude towards challenges and setbacks also shape their mindset and resilience. It is our responsibility to be mindful of our actions, as they shape the values and character of the next generation. Through our influence, we can inspire children to become compassionate, responsible, and confident individuals.

In addition to being positive role models, we also need to actively engage with children and provide them with opportunities to learn and grow. This can be done through activities such as reading, playing games, and exploring nature. By spending quality time with children, we can foster their curiosity and imagination, and help them develop a love for learning. It is also important to listen to their thoughts and feelings, and encourage them to express themselves in a healthy and respectful manner. By doing so, we create a safe and supportive environment where children can thrive and realize their full potential.

We all have a personal scale of gratitude, and it is extremely important. In order to keep the mentors we find in our lives, we need to show them they are appreciated. Their presence, their teaching, and their love are appreciated. This can be done by mailing them a card every year, just to show them you care and keep the relationship active.

Children are like sponges, absorbing every bit of information and behavior they see around them. As adults, it is our responsibility to ensure that they are exposed to positivity and kindness. We need to teach them to respect others, appreciate the little things in life, and have a growth mindset. By doing so, we help them develop into mature and responsible individuals who can contribute positively to society. It is important to set a good example for children, as their future is in our hands. Therefore, let us be mindful of our actions and words and strive to be a positive influence in their lives. Together, we can create a better tomorrow for our children and the generations to come.

In conclusion, our actions and behavior as adults have a profound impact on children. By being positive role models, actively engaging with children, and providing them with opportunities to learn and grow, we can help shape the values and character of the next generation. Let us take our responsibility seriously and strive to be the best versions of ourselves, for the sake of our children and the future of our world.

Chapter 4

The Beauty of Love: A Complex and Multifaceted Emotion

Love can be difficult to define, as it is a multifaceted and complex emotion. It is a profound affection and attachment to someone, often accompanied by a strong sense of care and concern. Love can exist in various forms, such as the love between family members, romantic love between partners, or even the love for a hobby or passion. It is a powerful force that can bring immense joy and happiness, but also cause pain and heartbreak. Love is built on a deep emotional connection and understanding, rather than just physical attraction. It is a selfless and unconditional feeling that compels individuals to prioritize the happiness and well-being of their loved ones, often above their own.

Love is not always easy. It requires effort, patience, and understanding, as well as compromise, sacrifice, and sometimes even letting go. However, the benefits of love far outweigh the challenges. Love brings a sense of purpose and meaning to life, and it allows individuals to experience a sense of belonging and connection with others. Love can inspire creativity, compassion, and empathy, and help individuals overcome adversity and find strength in the face of challenges. It is a universal language that transcends boundaries and has the ability to unite people from diverse cultures and backgrounds.

However, it is important to note that love is not always expressed through actions. We must put thought into what we define as love and its various forms. Do we love things or people? Does love mean forgetting one's mistakes or distancing ourselves from them until we are ready to move forward with a loving heart? The mismatch in actions and words regarding love causes confusion, especially for young children.

To build our understanding of love, we must change our definition of it and strive to embody its qualities in our daily lives. Love builds, nurtures, and protects. It is forgiving and forgetting at the same time. Love builds legacies and strong family bonds that help us all succeed. By doing so, we can create a better world for ourselves and those around us – one that is filled with the beauty and power of love.

Heal Over Time

Chapter 5

The Importance of Respect in Human Interaction

Respect is an essential component of human interaction that recognizes and appreciates the worth, dignity, and rights of others. It involves treating people with kindness, empathy, and consideration, while acknowledging and valuing their opinions, beliefs, and boundaries. By fostering positive relationships, respect creates a sense of harmony and trust within families, forming the foundation for a peaceful and loving support system that values each other equally.

Respect is a virtue that requires self-awareness, open-mindedness, and a willingness to learn and grow. By listening to others with the intent to understand, we show respect and set an example for others to follow. It is a valuable asset that can be instilled in us from a young age or developed over time.

Respect begins with ourselves, as we must respect our own boundaries, values, and beliefs before we can expect others to do the same. This means setting healthy boundaries, communicating needs effectively, and being open to constructive feedback and criticism in a respectful manner.

Respecting others' cultures and traditions is also essential, as everyone has a unique background, experiences, and perspectives. By embracing diversity, we can learn from one another and grow as individuals and as a family.

Respect also involves being mindful of our impact on the environment. We must treat the planet with the same level of care and consideration as we do for each other. This means reducing waste, conserving resources, and being mindful of our carbon footprint.

It is your responsibility to keep the negative out of your mind. A wise man once said to me, "What other people say about you is none of your business." There have been many times in my life where I had to stop someone from telling me what someone said about me because if they did not say it to me, it was not meant for my ears.

On another note, when we listen to someone talking about others talking negatively about others, we condone that behavior, and it may also serve as a confirmation if you agree to listen. You have a choice about which conversations you entertain and don't. I have learned that when others talk about people negatively to you and smile in their face, consider yourself as a future topic of their negative gossip.

It's important to understand that we have control over our thoughts and emotions. We can choose to let negativity consume us or we can choose to block it out and focus on the positive. It's not always easy, but it's necessary for our mental and emotional well-being. It's also important to remember that when someone speaks negatively about others in our presence, we have a responsibility to shut it down. Not only does it perpetuate negativity, but it also creates an atmosphere of distrust and toxicity. We can choose to be the person who lifts others up instead of tearing them down, and in doing so, we can create a more positive and supportive environment for ourselves and those around us.

It can be challenging to express your discomfort and avoid discussing a sensitive topic with someone. However, it is crucial to communicate your feelings and establish healthy boundaries in your relationships. Remember, it takes courage to be honest about your needs.

In conclusion, respect is a crucial aspect of our daily lives and interactions that requires us to be empathetic, open-minded, and self-aware. Remember, it's okay to express your discomfort and put yourself first. With practice and patience, we can cultivate a positive mindset that will serve us well in all areas of life. By practicing respect, we can create a world that values and celebrates differences and promotes mutual understanding and cooperation.

Chapter 6
The Ripple Effect of Grace and Forgiveness

Extending grace to others means offering kindness, forgiveness, and understanding, even in challenging situations. This involves showing empathy and compassion, acknowledging their struggles and shortcomings, and choosing not to hold their mistakes against them. Giving grace requires us to let go of resentment, anger, and judgment, and instead, offer love and acceptance. It means offering a second chance, a listening ear, and a helping hand, without expecting anything in return. By giving grace, we put ourselves in the other person's shoes, look beyond their actions, and understand their intentions. It requires patience and humility, recognizing that we too make mistakes and need grace from others. Ultimately, giving grace allows for healing, growth, and building stronger and more meaningful relationships.

Forgiveness is a crucial aspect of our personal growth and emotional well-being. It helps us release anger, resentment, and hurt that we carry within ourselves. When we forgive, we free ourselves from the chains of negativity and find inner peace. Holding grudges only weighs us down and prevents us from moving forward in life. Forgiveness benefits not only ourselves but also promotes healthy relationships with others. It opens the door to reconciliation, understanding, and healing. By forgiving, we demonstrate compassion and empathy, fostering an environment of love and acceptance. It is through forgiveness that we can break the cycle of pain and create a brighter future for ourselves and those around us. Therefore, it is crucial to embrace forgiveness as a powerful tool for personal growth and a path towards inner harmony.

As we go through life, we may unknowingly reflect our parents' mannerisms, beliefs, and behaviors. It is a fascinating phenomenon that shows how our parents' influence seeps into us at a subconscious level. Sometimes, it may be in the way we communicate, the values we hold dear, or the choices we make. Whether we realize it or not, our parents' presence looms in the background of our actions and decisions, shaping who we are and how we perceive the world. This intergenerational transfer of traits highlights the powerful bond between parents and children, even when we strive to be our own individuals. It reminds us that our parents' legacy lives on within us, guiding us in ways we may not always recognize.

Forgiving our parents is crucial for our healing process. Our parents play a significant role in shaping our lives and molding our perspective on the world. However, they are not immune to mistakes and shortcomings. It is through forgiveness that we can release the pain and resentment that may have accumulated over the years. Forgiving our parents is not about condoning their actions or forgetting the hurt they may have caused; rather, it is a powerful act of self-love and liberation. By acknowledging their fallibility and choosing to let go, we allow ourselves to heal and move forward towards a more fulfilling life. The healing process is not linear, but by embracing forgiveness, we can find solace and create space for growth and transformation.

Forgiveness is a powerful virtue that can mend broken relationships and heal deep wounds. When our parents show us forgiveness, it teaches us empathy, understanding, and compassion. We realize that everyone makes mistakes and that it is possible to move past them. This invaluable lesson is then passed down to our children, as we strive to create a nurturing and forgiving environment for them. By forgiving our parents, we break the cycle of resentment and anger, allowing our children to witness forgiveness in action. They learn that forgiveness is not a sign of weakness, but rather a sign of strength and growth. In turn, they learn to forgive us, knowing that we too are imperfect beings.

Giving grace to others can be a challenging task, especially when we feel wronged or hurt. However, it is important to remember that giving grace is not about excusing someone's behavior or letting them off the hook. It is about acknowledging their humanity and choosing to respond with kindness and compassion. It is about recognizing that we all make mistakes and that forgiveness is a powerful tool for healing and growth. We inspire others to do the same and create a more forgiving and compassionate environment which we all can thrive. Therefore, let us embrace forgiveness as a powerful tool for personal growth and a path towards inner harmony.

In conclusion, extending grace and forgiveness to others and ourselves is a powerful act of self-love, healing, and growth. It requires patience, empathy, and humility, but the rewards are invaluable. When we forgive, we release ourselves from the chains of negativity and find inner peace. When we extend grace to others, we create a ripple effect of positivity and love in the world. As we navigate through life, let us embrace forgiveness and grace as powerful tools for personal growth and healing.

Heal Over Time

Chapter 7
The Importance of Spirituality and Finding One's Purpose in Life

Spirituality is a deeply personal and individual journey that goes beyond religious beliefs or practices. It is a quest for meaning, purpose, and connection to something greater than oneself. It encompasses the exploration of one's inner self, seeking inner peace, and understanding the fundamental questions of existence. It is a path towards self-discovery, self-awareness, and self-transcendence. Spirituality is about embracing and cultivating virtues such as compassion, gratitude, and forgiveness. It involves developing a sense of mindfulness and being present in the moment. Spirituality is not limited to any specific religion or dogma; rather, it is a universal and inclusive concept that recognizes the inherent spirituality in all human beings. It allows individuals to connect with their higher selves, with others, and with the world around them, ultimately leading to a sense of happiness., harmony, and purpose in life.

Finding one's purpose is a journey that often starts with self-reflection and introspection. It involves delving deep into one's passions, values, and strengths to understand what truly brings meaning and happiness. to their life. It requires asking oneself thought-provoking questions, exploring various paths, and being open to new experiences. It is through this process of self-discovery that a person begins to uncover their unique purpose. It may not happen overnight, and there may be moments of doubt and uncertainty along the way. However, with perseverance and a willingness to embrace change, individuals can align their lives with their purpose. Once discovered, living with purpose brings a sense of direction, motivation, and joy, as one feels their actions are contributing to something greater than themselves.

Finding one's purpose in life is a journey that takes intentional thought and can take time and effort. It requires introspection and reflection on one's values, passions, and strengths. It is not always easy to know what we want to do with our lives, but by listening to our inner voice and seeking guidance from a higher power, we can gain clarity and direction.

Prayer and meditation are powerful tools that can help us connect with our higher selves and tap into our intuition. They allow us to quiet our minds and tune out the distractions of the world, so we can focus on what truly matters. By spending time in silence and contemplation, we can gain insights into our deepest desires and aspirations.

It is important to remember that our purpose in life is not necessarily tied to our career or material success. It can be as simple as spreading kindness, being a good friend or family member, or making a positive impact on the world in some way. Whatever it may be, finding our purpose can bring a sense of fulfillment and joy that cannot be found through external achievements alone. It is important that we act in accordance with our ethical standards and treat others with respect and fairness. As we move forward we intentionally make decisions and choices that prioritize the well-being and welfare of others, even in difficult situations. It is about doing what is right, even when it is not the most convenient or popular option. It is not merely about following rules or laws, but rather an inner sense of integrity and a commitment to upholding moral values. It is the foundation for a just and harmonious family, promoting empathy and compassion.

When we find our purpose, we gain a sense of direction and meaning in our lives. We become more focused and motivated, and we are better able to overcome challenges and setbacks. However, it is important to note that our purpose may change over time, as we grow and evolve as individuals. It is okay to reassess our goals and priorities periodically and make adjustments as needed.

In addition to prayer and meditation, seeking guidance from mentors or trusted advisors can also be helpful in finding our purpose. These individuals may have insights, experiences, and perspectives that can help us gain clarity and perspective on our own journey.

Ultimately, finding our purpose in life is a journey that requires patience, self-reflection, and openness to new experiences and perspectives. By staying true to ourselves and our values, and by seeking guidance along the way, we can discover the unique contribution we are meant to make in the world

Once we have discovered our purpose, it is important to take action to align our lives with it. This may involve setting goals, making changes to our daily habits or routines, and taking risks to pursue our passions. It may also involve letting go of things that no longer serve us or that are in conflict with our values.

Living with purpose requires a certain level of courage and resilience. It means being willing to step outside of our comfort zone, to face our fears and doubts, and to persevere through challenges and setbacks. However, the rewards of living a purposeful life are immeasurable. We experience a greater sense of contentment, joy, and connection to something greater than ourselves.

Living a life with purpose is not just about finding our own meaning and fulfillment, but it also involves making a positive impact on the world around us. It is about recognizing the interconnectedness of all living beings and taking responsibility for our actions. We can also promote empathy and understanding by listening to and learning from people with different backgrounds and perspectives. By living a purposeful life, we can inspire others to do the same and create a ripple effect of positive change. In essence, living with purpose is not just about personal growth but also about making a meaningful and lasting impact on generations to come.

In conclusion, finding our purpose in life is a journey of self-discovery that requires patience, introspection, and a willingness to embrace change. By connecting with our higher selves, seeking guidance from mentors, and taking action to align our lives with our purpose, we can live a more meaningful and fulfilling life. Remember that our purpose may evolve and change over time, and that is okay. What matters most is that we stay true to ourselves and our values, and that we continue to pursue our passions with courage and resilience.

Chapter 8
Taking Control of Your Future

As children, we may have experienced traumatic events that have left physical, emotional, and psychological scars. These experiences can be a range of things such as physical or sexual abuse, neglect, witnessing violence, or experiencing the loss of a loved one. Such traumas can disrupt our sense of safety, trust, and attachment, leading to a wide range of symptoms and difficulties.

However, it's essential to recognize that we have the power to shape our future and stop dysfunctional traits in our family. Setting goals and working towards achieving them is one way to do this. Having a clear vision of what we want to accomplish allows us to make conscious decisions and take actions that align with our desired outcome. Taking responsibility for our actions and choices is also crucial in determining the direction of our future. This involves recognizing the consequences of our decisions and learning from past mistakes to make better choices in the future. Additionally, we can exert control over our future by continuously learning and acquiring new skills. By investing in personal growth and development, we expand our opportunities and increase our chances of success.

Life is full of challenges, some of which may seem insurmountable. However, it's important to accept these adversities and find ways to overcome them. Embracing our unique story, both the good and the bad, is a part of our journey. Instead of dwelling on the negatives, we should focus on the positive aspects of our life. Amidst the ebb and flow of life, we are blessed with experiences that shape our very being. With each passing moment, we grow, learn, and develop into the person we are meant to be. Remember to be kind to yourself and take things one day at a time. With a positive outlook and a determined mindset, we can conquer anything that comes our way.

It's important to remember that seeking professional help is always an option and can greatly aid in the healing process. Therapy can provide a safe and supportive space for individuals to process their past experiences and develop healthy coping mechanisms. It can also help individuals gain a deeper understanding of themselves and their behaviors.

Finally, staying open-minded and adaptable is essential. Life is unpredictable, and things may not always go as planned. By being flexible and willing to pivot when necessary, we allow ourselves the opportunity to grow and learn from new experiences. While we may not have control over our past experiences, we do have control over how we choose to move forward. By setting goals, taking responsibility for our actions, continuously learning and growing, embracing our unique story, loving and forgiving ourselves, we can continue to heal and shape our future in a positive and fulfilling way.

Heal Over Time

Chapter 9

The Importance of Taking Action

Doubt can be a powerful force that hinders us from achieving our goals. It is the nagging voice in our heads that questions our abilities and fuels our insecurities. However, allowing doubts to hold us back can be detrimental to our progress and growth. In this article, we explore the importance of taking action, even when doubts arise.

Don't adopt others' doubts and fight through your own. Doubt is a natural part of the human experience, but there is a great sense of achievement when you do the very thing you thought was going to be hard to accomplish. To overcome doubt, we must challenge our negative self-talk, embrace our strengths, and believe in our ability to adapt and thrive.

One effective way to overcome doubt is by creating an action plan. An action plan is a detailed roadmap that outlines our goals, objectives, and the steps we need to take to achieve them. It acts as a guide, providing us with clarity, direction, and focus on how we can make our dreams a reality. With an action plan, we can break down our goals into smaller, manageable tasks, allowing us to stay organized and motivated along the way. It helps us prioritize our actions, allocate resources effectively, and track our progress. By having a well-defined action plan, we can overcome obstacles, stay committed to our aspirations, and ultimately create the life we desire. It empowers us to take control of our future, making every decision and effort purposeful and intentional. In essence, an action plan in life is our blueprint for success.

Taking action, despite our doubts, allows us to confront and challenge them head-on. It enables us to gather valuable experiences and learn from our mistakes. Taking action also builds confidence and resilience, as it shows our commitment and determination to succeed. By pushing through our doubts and taking consistent steps towards our goals, we open ourselves up to new possibilities and opportunities. Even if the outcome might not be exactly as expected, the process of taking action will undoubtedly lead us closer to our desired outcome. So, let us embrace our doubts, but not let them hinder us from taking the necessary actions towards achieving our goals.

Remember, doubts are natural and inevitable, but they should not prevent us from living our best lives. By challenging our doubts, creating an action plan, and taking consistent steps towards our goals, we can overcome obstacles and achieve success.

Heal Over Time

Chapter 10
Choose Happiness

Happy people just seem to have it all, right? But what's the secret sauce that makes them so successful? Researchers have been pondering this question for ages. Are they happy because they're successful, or successful because they're happy? The upbeat attitude of happy people drives them to be more productive and motivated, leading to greater success in all aspects of their lives. Plus, their strong social networks and positive relationships are a big boost.

But, hold on! Could it also be that happy people are more comfortable with failure? Sometimes the fear of not being perfect can be a real project-staller. Happy people, on the other hand, have a growth mindset, so they see failures as opportunities to learn and grow, not reasons to give up. They're not afraid to embrace failure and use it as an experience to move forward and achieve greater success.

Another reason happy people are so successful is that they're better at managing stress. While we all experience stress, happy people have better coping mechanisms, which keeps them focused and productive in challenging situations. We all want to be around happy people because smiles are contagious.

But wait, there's more! Happy people also have a stronger sense of purpose and meaning in their lives, which keeps them motivated and focused on their goals. They're open to new ideas and experiences, which leads to greater creativity and innovation.

So, while the relationship between happiness and success is a complex one, it's clear that cultivating happiness can have a positive impact on all areas of our lives. So, let's keep smiling and chasing our dreams!

Heal Over Time

Chapter 11
Be Supportive

We've all experienced a time when we needed support from friends and family, especially during significant events like weddings and graduations. If we want to increase the level of support we receive, we must make an effort to show up for others as well.

Support comes in various forms, and it's important to remember that it's not always physical. Sometimes, a kind word or a thoughtful gesture can make all the difference. Moreover, support should not be limited to big moments only. Checking in on someone during tough times or lending a listening ear can be incredibly supportive.

Approaching support with an open mind and an open heart is vital because everyone has unique needs and ways of coping. We must respect and honor those differences. And if you're unsure how to support someone, don't be afraid to ask. Asking how you can help can be the most supportive thing you can do.

Ultimately, being supportive is all about creating a culture of kindness and compassion. When we show up for others, we create a ripple effect of positivity that can spread far and wide. We must remember to share the information, which gives others to opportunity to support. Let's all commit to supporting one another, not only in the significant moments but also in everyday life. Together, we can create a world that is kinder, more loving, and more supportive for all.

Chapter 12
Embracing The Natural Cycle Of Life And Death

Death is an inevitable part of life. As permanent as it may feel when you loose someone you love, it is not. I had to ask myself after my daughters death, if I was crying for her or crying for myself. I was mourning the future I had envisioned for us, including the grandchildren I would never get to meet. My tears also reflected the agony of witnessing her last moments, as I could do nothing to alleviate her pain or alleviate her fears except to assure her that God was with her and everything would be alright.

At this point in my life, I do believe that the way we die is a testament to how we lived. If we live a life full of love, kindness, and generosity, we will likely die surrounded by loved ones, with memories of a life well-lived. On the other hand, if we live a life filled with anger, hate, and bitterness, we will likely die alone, with regrets and a sense of emptiness. It is important to remember that the way we live our lives has a direct impact on how we leave this world.

This experience has opened me up to giving others grace. To give someone grace is to show them kindness and compassion, even when they may not deserve it. It is about extending forgiveness and understanding, and choosing to see the best in others. Giving grace is about recognizing that everyone makes mistakes and has their own struggles, and it is our responsibility to offer support and empathy, rather than judgement and criticism. So let us all strive to live a life filled with joy, love, and positivity, so that when our time comes, we can leave with peace and contentment in our hearts and in the hearts of our loved ones.

Heal Over Time

It took me a long time to come to terms with the fact that death is a natural part of the cycle of life. It's a painful truth, but it's something that we all have to face at some point in our lives. It's okay to grieve and feel sad, but it's also important to remember that our loved ones who have passed away would want us to keep living our lives to the fullest. They would want us to find joy and happiness in the memories that we have shared with them. Just as I would want my loved ones to. It's not easy, but we have to try to focus on the good times and the love that we shared with the ones we have lost. In that way, they will always live on in our hearts and memories.

It's important to also remember that everyone grieves differently. Some people may want to talk about their loved ones and share stories, while others may prefer to keep to themselves. There's no right or wrong way to grieve, but it's important to find healthy ways to cope and seek support if needed. Whether it's through therapy, talking to friends and family, or joining a support group, there are resources available to help us navigate through the pain of losing someone we love. In the end, the most important thing is to know we can keep their memory alive and honor their legacy by living our lives with love and grace.

Heal Over Time

Chapter 13
You Get Out
What You Put In

Whether it's with friends, siblings, children, parents, or colleagues, every interaction with others is a relationship. Nurturing valued relationships is essential, as they are based on mutual benefit and understanding.

Communicating for the purpose of understanding someone else vs being understood is always going to benefit the goal. Selfless attitudes build relationships.

When we communicate with the intention of understanding someone else, we open ourselves up to new perspectives and experiences. It allows us to empathize with the other person, even if we don't necessarily agree with their point of view. This type of communication fosters a sense of connection and builds trust in relationships.

Conversely, when we communicate solely for the purpose of being understood, we run the risk of coming across as selfish or closed-minded. This approach can hinder our ability to build meaningful relationships with others, and may ultimately limit our personal growth and development.

By adopting a selfless attitude in our communication, we can create a more positive and inclusive environment where everyone feels heard and valued. This can lead to stronger relationships and a greater sense of community, both in our personal and professional lives. So the next time you find yourself in a conversation, try to approach it with the goal of understanding the other person, and see how it can benefit both you and your relationships.

You invest time and energy into building a strong foundation of trust and respect. You communicate openly and honestly, and you actively listen to others needs and concerns. You make an effort to show appreciation and gratitude, and you celebrate each other's successes.

Nurturing a relationship requires effort, communication and patience. It involves actively listening to the other person, showing empathy and understanding, and being willing to compromise. When you value a relationship, you prioritize it and make time for it in your life. You also understand that relationships are not always easy and may require work to overcome challenges or conflicts. By investing in your relationships, you can create your village and we all know that it take a village to raise a child. When we intentionally work towards these goals we indirectly set our children up for success. The energy and love that you put into your village create a bond that can withstand the test of time.

Heal Over Time

Chapter 14
The Importance of Self-Forgiveness

It is important to forgive oneself. One must learn to forgive themselves. Even though it sounds easy it may be a difficult task for some. Every mistake made has served as a lesson, shaping who you are today. It is important to acknowledge and take responsibility for your actions, but dwelling on them can lead to unnecessary guilt and shame.

Remember that everyone makes mistakes, and it is through these mistakes that we learn and grow.

To forgive yourself, start by practicing self-compassion. Treat yourself with the same kindness and understanding that you would offer a friend who made a mistake. Remind yourself that you are human and imperfect, and that these imperfections make you unique and valuable. We are all bound to stumble at some point in our lives. What is most important is how we choose to respond to those mistakes that truly defines us.

Another helpful step is to focus on the present moment and the future. Instead of dwelling on past mistakes, try to focus on what you can do now to improve and move forward. Set goals for yourself and take positive steps towards achieving them.

Your mistakes are not in vain. Sharing the mistakes you have made can be beneficial to others. By sharing, you could help someone avoid making the same mistake, which can be a powerful impact in the grand scheme of things and touch more lives in a positive way than you can imagine.

Forgiving yourself is a process that may take time and effort. But with patience and self-love, it is possible to let go of the past and embrace a more positive future. It's easy to get caught up in the past, to dwell on the things we wish we had done differently. But holding onto regret only serves to weigh us down. Instead, we must learn to forgive ourselves for our past mistakes and to use them as opportunities for growth and learning. By forgiving ourselves, we can let go of the past and move forward with clarity and purpose. We can use our mistakes as valuable lessons to guide us towards a brighter future. So take a deep breath, let go of any regrets, and embrace the person you have become today.

Self-forgiveness is not just about letting go of guilt and shame, but also about accepting yourself fully and unconditionally. It's about recognizing your worth and believing that you deserve forgiveness and happiness. So be kind to yourself, practice self-compassion, and trust that you are capable of growth and change. With time and effort, you can learn to forgive yourself and move forward with confidence and positivity. We can all strive to be a better person than we were yesterday.

In conclusion, as we go through life, we inevitably encounter experiences that leave us feeling hurt, angry, and resentful. These negative emotions can build up over time and make it difficult for us to move forward. However, the power of love and forgiveness can help us heal and find peace.

When we choose to forgive ourselves and those who have wronged us, we release ourselves from the burden of carrying around that pain. It doesn't mean that we condone their actions or forget what happened, but rather that we choose to let go of the negative emotions that are holding us back. Love, both for ourselves and for others, can also be a powerful healing force. When we treat ourselves with kindness and compassion, we create a positive self-image and attract more positivity into our lives.

Over time, with the help of love and forgiveness, we can heal from even the most painful experiences. It may not happen overnight, but with patience and persistence, we can find the peace and happiness we deserve.

Personal Action Plan & Notes

_____

_____

_____

_____

_____

_____

_____

_____

www.ingramcontent.com/pod-product-compliance
Lightning Source LLC
Chambersburg PA
CBHW071928020426
42331CB00010B/2771